Beginner's Guide to Google AdWords

TABLE OF CONTENTS

DISCLAIMER

ABOUT THE AUTHOR

John Slavio is a programmer who is passionate about the reach of the internet and the interaction of the internet with daily devices. He has automated several home devices to make them 'smart' and connect them to high speed internet. His passions involve computer security, iOT, hardware programming and blogging.

Introduction: What are Google AdWords?

If you're reading this, you're probably just starting out with a website you're looking to monetize, or you're hoping to use Google AdWords to increase your business revenue through advertising. Google AdWords is the main source of revenue for the tech giant Google, which has brought standard bearers and advances in search engines, e-mail systems, calendars, advertising, and all sorts of web and web placement codes and services. If you're reading this e-book, you very likely have used a Google product in the last hour of your life. And yet, AdWords is the highest earner for Google. What's that all about?

Google AdWords is both very simple and endlessly complex. In its most basic form, an advertising firm, a corporation, or a small business pays for a few lines of text called "advertising copy" (or simply just "copy") to be displayed on the web. You have seen Google AdWords on your favorite fashion websites, sports websites, online stores, blogs, and even on Google itself.

If you've ever seen these ads, you might have noticed that they're based on your interests – or, at least, what you've been searching on the web. If you've been looking up light bulbs or lighting fixtures and then you find yourself on a home improvement blog, you might see ads in the bottom left or right corner for lamp warehouses, discount halogen bulbs, and longer-life incandescent bulbs for your home office. It's not magic – it's an algorithm. These ads show up for you partially because of the Google AdWords system. When your search or browse on the web, sites drop "cookies" to track user data. Keywords that the advertiser has selected match up to your browsing history. These tiny bits of information are transmitted into the AdWords algorithm, and that's how an online lamp outlet store ad ended up on the blog you're reading. That's how AdWords works for end users.

For businesses and advertisers, we see the other side of the AdWords model. Advertisers pay to have their copy placed within this algorithm by the keywords they predefine. For example, if you're a shoe store in Philadelphia, your predefined keywords might be "shoe store," "shoe store Philadelphia," or "best shoe store in Philadelphia." There are an infinite amount of combinations, and advertisers often test efficacy by trial and error. After it's determined what ad copy will be used, these ads are ready to appear on Google's partner sites and other participating websites. There are several ways that Google makes money from this practice, but in its most basic sense, a click on the ad generates revenue for Google. In 2012, AdWords revenue alone netted the web giant $43.7 billion – almost 96% of Google's revenue. Who thinks advertising isn't powerful now?

How advertisers pay for their ads is another complex story. AdWords offers the following: pay-per-click (PPC) advertising, cost-per-click (CPC) advertising, cost-per-acquisition advertising (CPA), cost-per-thousand impressions (CPM) advertising, and site targeted advertising. Site targeted advertising is used for banner ads on websites, text boxes, and media rich ads. Another form of advertising Google AdWords employs is re-marketing or re-targeting. We will go over these types of advertising more in depth in later chapters, but what's important to note is that there is typically no minimum or maximum that companies must spend. Google AdWords is imminently scalable.

Google AdWords has rightfully spawned an entire Internet marketing industry. There are companies now that specialize in navigating and simplifying the difficult job of managing AdWords accounts. Google provides some software for employees to use, the most popular of which is called AdWords Editor. As AdWords has exploded, credentialing, best practices, and consultancies have been formed and exploded on the scene. In the past 17 years, AdWords has grown exponentially. Clients used to pay a minimum monthly amount, and Google would manage their ad campaign internally. With the explosion of the Internet and e-business, there's no way that's possible now – hence the pop up of the cottage industry surrounding Google AdWords. And a cottage industry it is no more. There's a multi-billion dollar world surrounding the use and management of AdWords.

This e-book aims to help you navigate the sometimes confusing world of Internet marketing, specifically in the Google AdWords space.

We will walk you through the benefits of using AdWords, and the types of advertising you can do. We will show you how to set up an account and build a campaign. And finally, we will reveal to you the secrets of keyword selection, the power of ad descriptions, and the best conversion optimization techniques. When you're finished with this book, we're confident that you'll be ready to master AdWords for your business. We hope you'll re-visit this book as needed. It is intended to be a great resource.

Benefits of Using Google AdWords

What's so great about using Google AdWords? A lot, it turns out!

First, let's delve deeper into the types of focusing you can do with your payment methods. A variety of advertising methods and selections make Google AdWords a smart pick for almost anyone with a web presence! After you've determined your budget, you'll want to decide what kind of traffic your company needs to focus on. The majority of advertisers focus on clicks. Other popular focus areas are impressions, conversions, engagements, and video ad views.

Pay-Per-Click (PPC)

While there are many types of methods by which you can focus your AdWords bidding, the most popular is the pay-per-click (PPC) form of advertising. If your major advertising goal is to get people's eyes on your website, pay-per-click is for you. It's also a little known fact that having people click on your website through your pay-per-click ads can positively impact where you turn up in regular Google searches, called organic searches. There are other benefits to the pay-per-click model:

- **Your budget is under your control.** If you need to be in charge of your advertising budget to the dollar, pay-per-click Google AdWords is the smartest type of Internet marketing for you. The most important part of a lower advertising budget is excellent keywords. We will cover this in a later chapter.

- **You're paying for the interested people, not the passive readers.** Someone has to opt in to look at your website via a click. This is extremely straightforward, and can help keep costs down. Would you rather pay for a billboard, or pay for everyone that comes to your store as a result of your billboard?

- **It's easier to track efficacy.** You will know how effective your ad copy or images and placements are if you have analytics on the number of people who go to your site. It's also helpful to understand the keyword game – you can do a few inexpensive tests, and see which keywords "hit" better.

- **Real time results.** You can see the number of clicks on your page very quickly, usually within hours or a day of the click. Stay up to date on what's working, what's not, and how much traffic your ad is bringing in.

- **Targeted ads at targeted times.** Running a President's Day sale in your neighborhood? You can select your ads and keywords to reflect this. Google AdWords lets the pay-per-click advertisers utilize location targeting and delivery options. If you get specific with your location, Google AdWords can see to it that your ad gets in front of an audience. This works well for events, sales, and other hyperlocal deals.

Don't let this fool you into thinking that pay-per-click advertising is easy. It's best to have a distinct strategy – or to hire someone who knows how to implement a strategy that will work well for your business. You've got to be creative, have good marketing fundamentals, common sense, and push toward an understanding of the AdWords platform. It's not easy, but it's worth it!

Focusing on Impressions? Try Cost-Per-Thousand (CPM).

There's another way to advertise in Google AdWords that works very well for businesses hoping to increase their brand visibility or logo recognition. Cost per impression is a great way to get in front of people's eyes. Maybe you're a new startup, and conversions and clicks aren't your strong suit yet, because nobody knows who you are. That's where cost-per-thousand comes in.

You'll only pay for every 1,000 impressions (or, views) of your ad on AdWords. You pay a low fee, and are charged every time 1,000 more people have viewed your ad or logo. It's been said that for every

10 impressions, you will get one conversion – and that's per person. This means a potential customer has to see your name or logo about ten times before they will register you as a purchasing option. Ever wonder why the Coca-Cola logo is everywhere? Ever wonder why, instead of "soda pop," lots of people (especially in the southern United States) will just say, "I want to have a Coke." They might mean a Diet Coke, a Dr. Pepper, or a generic soda, but, to them, the words soda and Coke are interchangeable. That's good branding.

One of the major benefits of cost-per-thousand impressions advertising is that Google won't cycle out your ad for having a poor click-through rate. If you're focusing on logo recognition and branding, consider the cost-per-thousand model.

Other Benefits of AdWords

There are many other reasons besides the versatile payment structures to use Google AdWords. First and foremost, virtually all Google searches – some 90% – are for products or services. When you pay for AdWords, your website could be shot to the top of search results within your keywords. If your ad copy is well written, imagine the click-through rates and name recognition! When you bid on keywords within your industry or directly related to your service or products, it will feel great to see your name at the top of the search bar. And you only pay if people click!

Another fantastic benefit of Google AdWords is that you will receive your Ad Rank. If your Ad Rank is high enough, your website will also be shot to the top of relevant search results in Google. Additionally, learning your Ad Rank occurs in real time, while SEO (if done correctly) takes time to organically grow your web page's ranking in search terms. It will cost you some advertising dollars, but it's a shortcut of the highest order.

It's also known that Google AdWords conversions can, in some instances, be almost twice as likely as organic conversions through traditional search means. If your ad is designed to sell, you'll be at a distinct advantage over other pages. Keywords, of course, matter too.

In short, finding out what works for your business – and only paying to do it by the click – is perhaps the best thing about Google AdWords. But hyperlocal targeting, higher conversions that regular web traffic, and knowing your Ad Rank are added bonuses of this already advertiser-friendly business model. The numbers don't lie, and the numbers are on your side.

One last thing? **Your competition is using Google AdWords.** Why aren't you?

Setting Up An Account

Setting up your Google AdWords account isn't difficult, and it's free. You will not be charged for creating an account, and you will not be charged for creating advertisements if you're choosing the pay-per-click fee structure. You will only pay Google when your ad starts performing. How's that for confidence in their product?

Before you set up your Google AdWords account, you will need the following things:

- **A business website.** Even if it's basic, you need a web presence. Your AdWords customers won't have anywhere to click if you don't have a dedicated home on the web! Think of your company's website as your office on the Internet. You want to showcase what's best and most important about your company, and you want to keep things clean and tidy so it's easy to maneuver around your space. Simple company websites often perform better than those with lots of bells and whistles. Your #1 goal should be to make it easy for your customers to purchase from you – hopefully easier and more enticing than buying from your competition.

- **A business e-mail address.** While most companies will have an email address like John@This Company.Com, that won't always be the case. It's okay if you need to use your Gmail address, or some other e-mail service. What's most important is that it looks like (and is) a legitimate e-mail address that you use only for business. If you're running a trucking company, don't give out an e-mail address like John@KnittingCircle.Com. It will confuse your potential customers, and can make you look unprofessional. Your best bet is a dedicated e-mail address for your company, by your company.

If you don't have a business website, you can still advertise on Google AdWords, although this should only happen in very special cases. If you are one of these cases, Google AdWords Express can work as your marketing solution. You can create an ad and start advertising in under an hour. It is highly recommended, however, that you have some sort of web presence.

Opening your Google Account

Your business, not your person, will need a Google account to utilize Google AdWords. Creating a Google account gives you access to all of Google's features: Gmail, Calendar, and Google+. If you already have a Gmail account, but it's used primarily for personal business, it's highly recommended that you create a completely new account. It's easier for tax and audit purposes, and it's easier to compartmentalize your business and see your results. You can invite several people or employees to collaborate on your AdWords account. After you've set up your AdWords account, you can add them.

After you've created a Google account, you will enter the website address of your business. After you've signed in, you might see a recommendation to use Google AdWords Express. This might be an automatic recommendation based on the information about your company that you previously input. It's up to you which service you use. We suggest AdWords proper.

It's also best to verify your account. Security concerns are real, especially if you offer a hot product or deal with large sums of money or proprietary information. Use two-step authentication, make sure to designate a recovery e-mail address, and take any other verification steps Google prompts. Don't forget to use a completely unique password. Random numbers and letters are often best.

Once you've created your account, take some time to familiarize yourself with the platform as its currently available to you. Click around, read help articles, watch tutorials if you prefer, and just take a moment to see what the fuss is all about. AdWords will likely be one of the most powerful tools in your marketing arsenal – it's best to know the lay of the land well!

Building a Campaign

You've looked into AdWords, you've thought about the possibilities, and you're convinced this is the easiest, cheapest, and most profitable way to advertise your business online. You're probably right! After you've created your account and familiarized yourself with the AdWords platform a bit, it's time to build a campaign. Click on the "Create a new campaign" button inside your account. Here we go!

Name Your Campaign

There are a few options for your campaign type. For your first (and probably all) of your Google AdWords campaigns, selecting "Search Network Only" is the most highly recommended selection option. This means that your Google AdWords ad can show up next to or on top of search results when one of your keywords is activated through search. For example, if you own an ice cream store in Birmingham, and someone searches "ice cream Birmingham," your ad will likely come up – and hopefully front and center. The Google Network contains the Search Network. Google Network is the name of the complete bundle of webpages and apps where AdWords are authorized to appear. It's also best to un-check the box labeled "Include search partners." You will also need to name your campaign. This name is used for internal use only.

Where In The World Will Your Ads Be?

This gets pretty cool. You can focus in or out geographically when you're selecting the scope of your Google AdWords campaign. You can choose whole countries (for example, South Africa or Canada), regions of countries (like the Eastern United States), cities (such as Detroit or Paris), US states (such as Hawaii), provinces (such as Nova Scotia in Canada), and much more. If your ad is politically targeted or just hyperlocal, you can even select Congressional Districts within the United States! If you're a real stickler, you can designate latitude and longitude coordinates and a radius around a certain address or city. If you can find it on the globe and if they have Internet, you can advertise there on Google AdWords.

We recommend starting small, especially if you're working with a small business. Cities, states, and congressional districts might be your best bet. If you're trying to proliferate your online store, countries or continents might be more appropriate. It's up to you to zoom in or out on the globe, but if you're primarily located and looking to sell your wares in one geographic area, your money is best spent seeking that out.

Choosing Your Budget & Bid Strategy

There are two elements at play here: what's smartest for your business financially, and what works best for your marketing strategy. Luckily, both of those things can work together with Google AdWords.

While there are several automatic options for your bidding strategy, as an AdWords beginner with a smaller budget, you'll want to manually set your bid amount for clicks. This means that you've opted into the pay-per-click system. Choose the option titled, "I'll manually set my bid for clicks."

Next, you'll set your daily budget. Your daily budget is the upper limit – the maximum amount that Google can charge your for your Google AdWords per day. After you get started, and especially if you have savvy keywording and location targeting, it's very likely that you will hit your upper limit each day. Depending on your budget, cash flow, and preferences, you will be able to select whether you prefer to pay Google prior to your ads showing up on the web, after your ads are showcased, or simply set up for monthly payments. Some companies will be eligible for Google's company credit line through monthly invoicing, but it's best not to worry about that if you're a small business or if you're just starting out.

The best budgeting strategy is one that won't break the bank. It's hard to be more specific than that because companies have such differing marketing budgets, but sometimes it's not necessary. Don't put all your eggs in one basket, and make sure you're keeping an eye on your results before you up the amount you're spending. It's good to set a daily, weekly, and monthly budget. Once you can evaluate performance, then you can figure out what works for you going forward. But learning the Google AdWords platform doesn't have to be expensive! Even companies with modest budgets can increase their Ad Rank and show up next to keyword searches. And, if your ad doesn't perform well, Google will stop running it. No harm, no foul.

Creating Your Campaign

Last but not least, you'll create your first ad group. Here goes nothing! Your campaigns will be grouped together, and, when you're just starting out, people tend to group them by date. It's much more profitable for your analytics to group them by themes. Grouping your ads by location, seasonality, brand names or generic names, keyword matches, or based on your products and services will likely be your best method of segmenting your ads. When you're just starting out, aim to run no more than five ads per campaign. This will give you a taste of what's working and what isn't.

Now you're ready to create your first ad!

Inserting Keywords

Although we'll cover keywords strategy next, it's important to know how to add your keywords to your AdWords account. The best strategy is to start with a few hyper-relevant keywords and expand out from there. There's no need to use hundreds of keywords at the beginning. Your ads will get lost in the shuffle.

Know Your Maximum Cost-Per-Click

Google uses the term "Default Bid," but this is your maximum cost-per-click. The most important thing to note here is that each of your keywords might render a completely different market. For example, while soccer shoes and knee-high socks are related, "cleats" and "tall socks" will conjure several different markets. When you're pasting in your keywords, connect them using the plus sign. Use brackets and quotation marks to see how many searches you will get per keyword.

And, finally, you'll enter your billing information into the Google AdWords system. Your ads will go live on the web as soon as your payment is verified.

Keyword Selection

The most important part of your ad is its copy – your words need to connect, and quickly. Your target customers will only be glancing at your ad, so you need to capture their attention and entice them to click, and quick. This can be extremely difficult, but we've got some tips that will help you write the best ads for your business. It all boils down to one thing: keywords.

The Rules of a Google AdWords Ad

It's all about the character limits, keywords, and what actually converts. These are the character counts you get per AdWord:

- Headline: 25 characters
- Line 1: 35 characters
- Line 2: 35 characters
- Display URL: 35 characters
- Final URL: 1024 characters

It's important to try to pack as much punch as you can in these few characters. You will need to use punctuation at the end of Line 1. It's important to think about your brand, your product, and your audience when crafting your ad copy. It's imperative that you include at least one keyword in your ad. Consumers need direction, even at a glance.

Planning Your Keywords

One of the most powerful tools in your arsenal is right there in your AdWords account. It's under the "Tools" menu. Select that menu to see the drop down list, and then select "Keyword Planner." Once you make this selection, Google will then prompt you with a question:

Where would you like to start?

You can search for new keywords, look at search volume data trends, or multiply keyword lists to find new keyword selections. The best use of the tool, and the easiest one to orient oneself for beginners, is to search for new keywords. For this, you'll use a phrase, website, or category.

Once you decide that this is the route you want to go, Google Keyword Planner will prompt you to enter one or more of the following pieces of information: your product or service, your landing page (which might just be your business's homepage), and a relevant category. It's imperative that you play with this for a little bit and learn how to do it right. This is perhaps the most important tool you will have at your disposal.

Your Product or Service

In this box, your purpose is to narrow down, not open up. If you're a baker, you don't want to enter things like "bakeries," or "cakes." Perfecting this search will come with a lot of trial and error, but entering three or less keywords here will be your best bet. If you can, stay within a niche market. Again, this is where you want to drill down. If you're a baker that makes vegan treats or has those options in your store, try "vegan desserts," or "dairy-free cookies."

Your Landing Page

This is fairly straightforward, especially if you are just starting out on the web. This field is mostly for AdWords users, but if your site is something specific, like "redsoccershorts.com," you might be able to glean a few keywords here. If you're going to skip a step, this is the one to skip. It definitely won't hurt you, and it's probably neutral on its chances of helping you in your keyword strategy and planning.

Your Product Category

This is another important field to be accurate in naming, because your answer will determine how and where to access Google AdWords' internal database. This is a massive keyword database that Google has been growing since the inception of AdWords, if not before. If you aren't getting a lot of help with the first option's drill downs, try using this feature. It's not necessary, but it could be an important step to finding you the best and most lucrative keywords for your product or service.

Keyword Results Page

Once you've done your targeting – which is choosing your location and negative keywords (these are covered in the next chapter) – you will be taken to the Keyword Results Page. The tabs across the top will read "Ad group ideas" and "Keyword ideas." While it might be tempting to spend all of your time on the Keyword ideas tab, make sure that you take some time to explore the Ad group ideas tab as well. It will also help you find effective and new keywords for your keyword and ad copy planning.

When you're looking at the Keyword ideas tab, you'll see your "Search Terms" across the top. This is the exact information you entered earlier. Next, you'll see "Keyword (by relevance)." This is the word or list of words that Google AdWords has deemed the closest and most relevant matches to your original search term. For example, if you typed in "basketball hoop," some of the keywords that will be returned are "basketball goals," "basketball backboard," and "basketball hoops for sale."

Your Keywords Planner will detail for you the average monthly searches of each proposed term, as well as the number of advertisers who are also bidding on the keyword. This is called "Competition." Also, take a look at the "Suggested Bid" portion of the matrix provided. While it may not look like much, there's actually a secret hidden in those numbers. Scan through the keywords once again. You'll see that the higher the bid, the more potential monetization the keyword has. And the more the suggested bid is listed for is a pretty good indicator of how lucrative your traffic from that keyword will be. You'll want to pick keywords with larger suggested bids.

These tools might help you choose some keywords or refine your ideas about what the best keywords for your ad copy are. Remember: you want to use at least one high-powered keyword in your ad, preferably in the headline. Choose keywords with higher bid rates and competition listings if you're looking for more conversions from your traffic due to AdWords clicks. Trust the numbers, and make your decisions based on the best performers.

The benefits of the Keyword Planner Tool are many. First, you're using Google's analytics for a Google program. There's every incentive to give you the most accurate and up to date results. If you do well, Google makes money. Second, you can see the historical performance of different keywords as well as the recent performance. You can see how lucrative it is relative to other keywords, and you can see what kinds of clusters your keywords come in. It also predicts traffic fairly accurately, with highly-ranked keywords consistently out-performing the lower ones.

Choosing Your Keywords

You've done your research. You know what words you want to use. But there are a few final tips that can help you decide whether a certain keyword belongs in your ad or not:

- **What word does your customer need to see to get them to click on your ad?** There's a bit of consumer psychology at play here. Consider listing out your business categories, and listing phrases or jargon that might emerge from a consumer operating in those spaces. Should you include brand names? Product names? Or should you keep it generic? These are all questions you'll need to know, and answer from the mind of your customer.

- **Target a specific demographic with a hyper-specific keyword.** The more specific your keyword, the more narrow your scope. While that can sound like a death sentence to some businesses, when you're gunning for a target demographic, this specificity is key. There's a balance to be had here. You don't want to limit the number of people you reach to too few, but you do want to target a certain group. Think about that group, and what words they want to see in an ad.

- **If you're completely unsure of your target demographic, or if your targets are broad, use general keywords.** It's not always recommended, but when you're first starting out, you might want to get a broad idea of your customer base. Who in the world would be looking for your business, anyway? To answer that question, you might want to keep it broad. It's a good experiment for your first AdWords campaign. A word of caution, however: because of their high conversion and click-through rate, some of these bids may be more competitive and therefore more expensive than more targeted keywords. Utilize this strategy as a test, and once you have data about your results, drill down to a more targeted keyword strategy.

- **Similar keywords should be in ad groups.** So many Google AdWords users underutilize their ad groups. If you group your keywords and ads into focused ad groups, you will naturally show more relevant ads to potential conversions and customers all over the web. The more keywords you have in an ad group, the less specific it can be. You don't want someone finding your ice cream parlor when they're searching for ice

31

sculptures! And you don't want to pay for clicks if those potential conversions aren't likely to buy. Keep like things together.

- **It's essential to use the right number of keywords.** Google AdWords recommends that, per ad group, you use between 5-20 keywords. Each ad group should be appropriately and narrowly themed; this is your opportunity to further target in a meaningful way. Google works hard for your keywords to match misspellings, plurals, and other variations. If you sell "coloring books" in the United States, but sell to people worldwide, your ad would likely come up when a child in London searches for "colouring books," for example.

Negative Keywords

If you've use Google Keyword Planner at all, you've probably seen the prompt for Negative Keywords. This can sound quite complicated at first. After all, you've just finished researching, learning, and refining all of your regular keywords. Now do you have to add another layer of confusion into the mix? The short answer here is: Yes.

But it doesn't have to be so difficult. Once you're in the Keyword Planner tool, and you're going through the steps, under the targeting vertical, you will see a geographic location, "Google and search partners," and finally, "Negative keywords."

Negative Keywords in the Keyword Planner Tool

They sound so sinister, don't they? But negative keywords are simply those that you specifically want to opt-out of advertising with. You can only use this feature in AdWords, and it can help you target the right customers by weeding out the non-potentials. Here, you can find and select the keywords you'd like to exclude.

For example, if you own a freelance writing business, and you want to advertise your content creation skills, one of your negative keywords might be "technical writing." You want to bid on the keywords like "freelance writer" and "web content writer," but you definitely don't want to get tasked with writing white papers. Find keywords to exclude here – such as "freelance technical writer," or "freelance tech manuals."

Negative Keywords in Your Ad Groups

The step-by-step process to adding negative keywords to your ad groups and campaigns is quick and hopefully painless. Once you're signed in to your account, click on the Campaigns tab. Then, of course, click on Keywords. This tab opens two tables, "Ad group level" and "Campaign level." You can add your negative keywords to either of these levels by click the button for "+Keywords" on top of each. You can add one negative keyword per line per field, just like adding "positive" keywords. Select which campaign or ad group you'd like to add them to, and then save your changes accordingly.

Additionally, in your regular keyword searches in the Keyword Planner Tool (as described and instructed in the last chapter), you can often find negative keywords by process of elimination. Say you have a list of keywords about basketball shoes for women. If you've done your research, you'll know that people searching for basketball shoes for women overwhelmingly use the search term "women" or "for women" in their Googling. When you're given your keyword list in the Keyword Planner Tool, read down the list – and simply eliminate any keywords that are gendered toward male basketball shoes. In fact, if you know your target audience will be searching for "women's basketball shoes," it's ok to eliminate any keywords that don't specifically reference that your customer is shopping for a female. Add those negative keywords to your ad or campaign group, and you will avoid advertising to those who aren't directly interested in your product.

It's interesting and perplexing how many companies – especially startups – don't invest the time and energy into the Google AdWords strategy to realize the return on investment that negative keyword targeting can bring. In fact, it's one of the most lucrative ways to increase your Ad Rank and AdWords efficacy, period. If you're just starting out with Google AdWords, or are looking for a way to refine your strategy, negative keywords can be an intelligent method by which to increase your ad's accuracy.

Ad Descriptions

The time has come: You're finally ready to create your first ad!

Keep in mind that there are character limits and certain strategies you'll want to employ in order to create the best ad. First, think about the psychology of your customer. Who are they? What do they want? Can you show them that they need it at a glance? You don't have long – typically just the blink of an eye's time. The good news is that it's possible to convert browsers into clickers using great ad copy.

You want high-performing ads that make an impact, and you've got to learn how to write them. The first rule of thumb is: Be creative. You're not only going to be competing with the search engine or webpage that your AdWords show up on, but you're also going to be listed right alongside between four and ten other competitors, depending on the device. That's a lot of ways to **not** convert browsers into clickers, and then clickers into customers. And it's true: Google AdWords don't get clicked millions time more than they do. But, they do. And that's the rub.

The Secret to a Winning Headline

You've got 25 characters to make yourself known as unique, viable, and create an urgency around purchases. Most of your competitors, especially those with lazy or no Google AdWords strategy, will be employing the use of dynamic keyword insertion. They're all bidding on the same keywords, and they're playing by the rules of the game. As a result of this, you can see when you're doing opposition research (or viewing your own ad!) that many of them all say the same thing. There's nothing different in "Discount Tooth Whitening" when both of your neighbors and their neighbors have used the same rhetorical devices. There's nothing unique about a large majority of the ads on Google AdWords. But, with your ads, all that's about to change.

The secret to a winning headline is **not** to give in to dynamic keyword insertion only, and to create a funky spin on that that catches the eye. For example, if your competition's headlines look like "Best Horse Stables in CT," you can easily flip that headline into a call to action. And you don't have to waste the space on the word "click." You do this by one method: Turning the headline into a question. This is one creative way to differentiate yourself from the others. Instead of "Best Horse Stables in CT," try "Need Horse Stables in CT?" This inversion of a statement into a question implies that your site has more of a solution. If you try to solve your customers' problems instead of simply sticking keywords in a declarative headline, you'll be head and shoulders above the companies around you – and their ads.

The question isn't always what you need, though. Your headline needs to be the simplest way to offer your customer a solution. For example, instead of "Recycling Bins for Sale," try "Get Your Recycle Bin Sale." The addition of an imperative sentence will psychologically trigger a perception of need in your customer. They'll be much more likely to click if you tell them to. It's a strange fact of the human brain, but it works well for the purposes of Google AdWords.

Your Body Text

You have 35 characters on each of two lines after your headline to further convince or explain to your customers what solution you can offer them by clicking on your site. Although your headline is the most important part of your advertisement, making sure your body text is on point is imperative, as well. If you haven't already done so in your headline, try some of these techniques for excellent AdWords copywriting:

- **Tell your customer what makes your different from the rest of the pack.** You only have one chance to stand out, and it's not going to be enough to look like the others. Tell your customer why you're unique. Do you offer free shipping? Do you have new items in stock? Are you an A-List brand that celebrities like? Were you seen on Oprah? Put out what makes you different – front and center.

- **Numbers are OK.** They might even be your friend. It's okay, and perhaps preferable, to include some notion of the price of your goods and services for your customers. People respond well when they think they have the information they need. Are your candlesticks on sale for $3.99? Is it a 2-Day Sale? Tell them that! Whether it's true as you build your business or not, the air of exclusivity is what drives many consumers. They want exclusive deals, the best prices, or the status of buying a limited edition.

- **Include a Call to Action.** Signpost for your customers! Do you want them to "Buy Now," "Call Today," or "Sign up?" Then tell them to. What good is letting them know there's a sale if you don't urge them to "Buy Now!" This might be the most important step of creating a Google AdWords ad and ad campaign: You've got to tell your customers what to do so they know they have the option to do it.

- **Make Your Ad Match Your Webpage or Landing Page.** Where are you sending them when they click? Instead of disorienting your customer with "Why did I click on this?" confusion, make sure that the copy you use in your ad is exactly or similarly present on your webpage or landing page. If you place an ad that says, "20% Off – Today Only – Canoes & Row Boats!" – make sure that text or something very similar is in big letters on the page you're sending your customers. Make it easy for them to identify you, and remind them of why they clicked your ad. Chances are, if they buy from you once, they will buy from you again – so you want to make sure you make it as simple as possible to get to your page. Decrease the need for them to have to "feel around." Direct, direct, direct!

- **Include at least one of your top performing keywords.** This one is self-explanatory. Make sure you get in front of the right eyes and let your customer know that you understand their needs by including the keyword that they've likely searched for. If they're looking for a dentist, your ad should read "Need Pearly Whites? Call #1 Dentist in Town!" Your ad should not read "Mike King DDS For All Your Tooth and Smile Needs." No one is going to feel confident clicking on that, even though it uses Dr. King's credentials to denote him as a dentist. Your Google AdWords ad should pass the "glance test." Customers should get excited about your product and know what they're paying (20% off, Sale, etc.) right off the bat. You only get a flash of a second to impress and delineate yourself from the others. Use a keyword to your advantage!

The Importance of Opposition Research

One of the best things you can do to improve your own headline writing is to look at the biggest names in your industry, then try to emulate the way they do their AdWords ads. You never have to re-invent the wheel in order to succeed. You probably used a template for your online store, or a familiar layout for your brick and mortar storefront. It's the same with AdWords. The biggest names in the business know what works. While you should strive to be unique in your advertising copy because you want to delineate yourself from other companies, look at the industry and thought leaders. Find their AdWords via keyword searching on Google.

Check out how they advertise seasonally, by event, and even by product. See what keywords they are using, and see if you can drill down to one more level of specificity. Watch for sales and emulate those – sometimes offering a tiny bit more of a bargain is the way to attract new and lasting customers. Always have your eye on your competition, and even those out of your league. Their strategies work for a reason, and – if they don't – you can learn from their mistakes.

Conversion Optimization Techniques

When you've got a product or service to sell and you're spending hard-earned advertising money on AdWords, you're going to want one thing: Results. The best ways to turn a browser into a customer can be mysterious, but with a little strategy and forethought – and a lot of practice! – you can convert the eyes on your page to paying patrons in no time.

Check out these winning conversion optimization techniques and tips for your Google AdWords advertisements:

- **Add value or a benefit to your CTA (Call to Action).** Instead of "Learn More," try "Yes! I want to travel cheaply."
  Sometimes people need to be led toward their purchasing decision, not hit over the head with it.

- **If you have a big number, show it off.**
  "50,000 Facebook fans can't be wrong."
  "10,000 people have bought them this month!"
  Using numbers makes you look popular, well-researched, and more reputable. Don't hesitate to throw a large number in your ad.

- **Use click trigger words.**

  "Only 20 left in stock!"

  "Buy Now, Pay Later!"

  Anything that makes your potential customer feel like they might miss out if they don't take action right now will increase your click through rates.

- **In a similar vein, add urgency to your headline.**

  "40 buys today. Supplies are limited!"

  Sometimes the hard sell works. The old adage, "think long, think wrong" is the crux of this conversion technique.

- **Ask for something smaller than you what you really want.**

  "Get a free estimate today!"

  "Check out our samples!"

  You want them to get interested in you. They might need to know who you are or why they should buy from you before they will click on a "Buy Now!" button.

- **Advertise your top sellers!**

  "Selling like hot cakes!"

  "See our top seller"

  "Most popular curling iron"

  Sometimes, running an ad completely about one product can work wonders for your conversion rate. Make sure you have a good targeting strategy, and that you can handle the amount of stock you need if suddenly everyone wants to buy from you.

- **Use emotion and emotive language.**

  "This will change your life!"

  "Customers love us – you will to!"

  "We bring the warmth of home to you."

  Making people feel something is a great way to connect. It's hard to do in so few words, but there are ways to tap the heart strings, even with Google AdWords.

- **Create an entire ad, just for your best selling product.**

  Featuring these are a great way to get clicks to your site. You can advertise your best sellers within an ad, but you can also do one sole focus product ad. Your keywords and location targeting needs to be tight, and you should be prepared for a dip in the sales of other products.

- **Don't ask them to buy, engage them further.**

  Try "See More," or "Sign up!" Sometimes, a Call to Action (CTA) doesn't work. But, if you can get them to your website, you can likely get them to convert. Make sure wherever you send them next is easy to navigate, simple, and has exactly what they want.

- **Is your product complex? Give more information.**
  E-Book offers or downloadable white pages are great for this! Once they've started learning about your product, customers will feel invested and will be much more likely to purchase from you!

- **Don't advertise your social media until it's popular.**
  It's not a good idea to link to your Facebook page from a Google AdWords ad until you have amassed a respectable following. Your social clout, or lake thereof, can drive otherwise excited customers away.

- **Have lots of landing pages.**
  When you make an AdWords ad, you'll want to link it to a landing page. If you have lots of landing pages for different ad campaigns, you're much more likely to convert leads into sales. More landing pages means more specialized offers, and more deals means more interest in your products. Studies show that if you have 10 or more landing pages on your site, you're 55% more likely to convert leads than those with 5 or less.

- **Use "loss aversion" tactics.**
  "Don't miss out!"
  "It's almost too late!"
  "Don't be the only one without one!"
  Make sure your potential customers know that if they

don't act now, they're going to lose out. People can be more highly motivated to avoid loss than they will be to gain something. It's a little psychological trick, yes – but it can lead to great conversions!

- **Do a human interest story.**

  "Meet the team!"

  "Check out the humans behind the world's best cars."

  You can link to your About Me page on your website, but it's better to have a landing page that's human interest heavy. Whether you are featuring customer testimonials or your staff, it's always best to showcase the human element of your business. This tactic should not be used as a primary optimization strategy for most companies.

- **Be specific.**

  "10% off if you buy 5 or more!"

  "Sizes 4-9 only!"

  It might sound like a no-brainer, but it's best to be specific with your ads. The more drilled down and detail oriented you can be, the more your most discerning lead will convert. Take the guess work out of their purchase, and let them know exactly what they're getting!

- **Think in bullet points.**

  If you're having a hard time connecting with customers,

brainstorm about your product – but really get down to the brass tacks. List possible pros and cons, and come up with a bulleted list of phrases or details that you want to promote. Turn those into copy, and make sure each one contains a keyword.

- **Don't use complicated jargon. Use plain English.**
  "We've got cardiac and pulmonary surgical instruments for sale or rent for in-home medical care and nursing homes." No way!

  Try this: "We're your home heart health supply."

  Avoid using words that string together or take up all your characters. There's usually a shorter way to say something complex, and in AdWords – brevity is key.

  Try to avoid jargon like this on your landing pages, too.

- **Avoid use of the word "Buy."**
  Consider replacing any instance of "buy" with a different word.

  "Reserve yours now!"

  "Pre-order today!"

  "Order yours for your success."

  "Send me some kitchen knives!"

  All of these avoid the hard sell, but they entice the reader into a purchase. Your lead may not know it, but they just became converted

- **Interesting back story? Showcase your origins!**

  "Created with love by former inmates."

  "Sustainably prepared on our family farm."

  "Made in Gambia by women paid a living wage."

  "Made in the USA!"

  If your customer wants to know the source, tell it to them. There's always a great story about how something gets manufactured or comes to be, and that can be part of your AdWords ad. Make sure there's a market for how you choose to source. Some people like to buy American, others want to know something's local, and others still like supporting economic development far across the globe.

- **Make a direct comparison to your competition.**

  "Our new tablet beat the iPad 5 to 1!"

  "Whiter smiles than Colgate"

  Let people know why you smoke the competition. Is it your low prices? Your quick shipping? Or your superior product? Direct selling like this can increase conversions at a really quick rate if you stick the landing!

- **Write in first person. Write in second person.**

  We're grouping these together because it really behooves you to try both of them. Run one Google AdWords ad in first person: "I want a free gift!"

Then, try writing the other in second person: "Your free gift is waiting."

Test and see what works better with your leads. Different industries and types of consumers respond to different tactics. Whichever one works best – that's the one to stick with!

- **Get negative.**

  "Never worry about your hair again!"

  "Worst hair? We got your fix right here!"

  Negative words perform better than positive ones in market research overall. Instead of saying, "best product ever," concentrate on what you're fixing by solving your consumers' problems. "Never be shy about smiling again!" will probably work better than, "Have white teeth. Always."

- **Action, action, action.**

  "Lose weight, feel great!" instead of "Our product helps you lose pounds."

  "Run faster, jump higher!" instead of "Ace bandages provides knee support."

  Your consumers want to feel like they are performing an action by buying your product or clicking on your site. Give them that reward. Action oriented copy is much more persuasive than its passive, lazy cousin.

- **Add a guarantee.**

    "You'll love it. We guarantee."

    "Money back guarantee."

    "Guaranteed coziest warm socks."

    When you provide a guarantee, you're showing someone that there's no risk to buying your product. This plays on consumers' need not to make the wrong choice.

    Guarantees also show that you've got integrity and will make good on

    your word. This increases your innate credibility and makes leads want to buy from you.

- **Be frank.**

    "We will save you money. Call us today!"

    "Finally, a hair spray you'll actually use."

    Sometimes, blunt honesty really is the best policy. Show people the most useful benefit that they'll get form buying your product or enlisting your services, and you will be sure to convert some no-nonsense buyers.

- **Get weird.**

    Your call to action statements don't have to be standard. Try something like, "I'm in!" instead of "Buy now!"

These are some of the best optimization techniques that you can use for Google AdWords copy. The beauty of them is that you can try one or more in different types of campaigns, and you will be able to see results quickly. One of the best features of pay-per-click advertising is the freedom to test what works best for you, and almost instantly know.

It's best to try different techniques related to the same product, sale, or event. This is where you can create an ad group (discussed in an earlier chapter) and try out several rhetorical and copywriting ideas to promote the same product to the same audience. If your ad doesn't convert browsers to clicks, you won't be paying for it, anyway.

Sometimes this strategy of trial and error is the best way to find out what works for you and your Google AdWords marketing strategy. Sometimes, you'll need to focus more on raw keywording and targeting ads. Both of these methods are excellent ways to learn more about how to advertise within your industry.

CONCLUSION

Google AdWords is a market giant, and it's not likely to significantly change in its innerworkings any time soon. The faster your business gets into the Google AdWords marketing game, the quicker you'll know how to craft ads for your leads, buyers, and consumers. It takes some time and a little bit of a budget, but businesses large and small can benefit from AdWords placement and smart online marketing strategy.

Whether you're trying to launch a new product, promote an event, or simply learn about Internet marketing, this guide is an excellent starting off point. What you'll need next is a personalized Internet marketing strategy, and a method by which to execute it. It's important to note that growing your business, and its advertising, can take time – especially if you don't have a dedicated staff to work on these issues full time. If you're doing it all on your own, you're likely to have to take it quite slow, and that's okay, too. Google AdWords can work at your speed and comfort level, and within your budget.

Internet marketing is a huge industry, and it's only expected to grow in future years. For the first time ever in 2016, Internet advertising dollars spent were more than those spent on television. Think about that – advertisements online as a whole can cost more than Superbowl ads!

If you've got any doubts about the power of your AdWords and their potential to help grow your business from the ground up, don't! Google AdWords is a staple of Internet marketing, and is only growing due to app culture and becoming more influential in our purchasing decisions. Whether you're working on branding, selling your wares, or looking to engage your users, Google AdWords is a great first step that will likely take you very far!

www.ingramcontent.com/pod-product-compliance
Lightning Source LLC
Chambersburg PA
CBHW071520210326
41597CB00018B/2828